Animal Detectives

by Wiley Blevins

Red Chair Press   Egremont, Massachusetts

Look! Books are produced and published by Red Chair Press:

Red Chair Press LLC   PO Box 333   South Egremont, MA 01258-0333

www.redchairpress.com

Publisher's Cataloging-In-Publication Data

Names: Blevins, Wiley

Title: Animal detectives / by Wiley Blevins.

Description: Egremont, Massachusetts : Red Chair Press, [2018] | Series: Look! books : Animals that help us | Interest age level: 004-007. | Includes Now You Know fact-boxes, a glossary, and resources for additional reading. | Includes index. | Summary: "You know that pets can be fun. But some dogs, horses, pigs, and more have important jobs to do. With Animals That Help Us young readers will discover how animals help us stay safe. Animal Detectives looks at how dogs, pigs, even bees are working with police to solve mysteries."--Provided by publisher.

Identifiers: ISBN 978-1-63440-316-0 (library hardcover) | ISBN 978-1-63440-364-1 (paperback) | ISBN 978-1-63440-322-1 (ebook)

Subjects: LCSH: Animals in police work--Juvenile literature. | CYAC: Working animals.

Classification: LCC HV8025 .B54 2018 (print) | LCC HV8025 (ebook) | DDC 363.25 [E]--dc23

LCCN 20179475558

Photo credits: Cover, 1, 7, 11, 21, 22: iStock; p. 3, 5, 23, 24: Shutterstock; p.9: © E.D. Torial/Alamy; p. 13: © ZUMA Press, Inc./Alamy; p. 15: © Nicko Margol; p. 17: © Christophe Boisvieux/Alamy; p. 19: © WENN Ltd/Alamy

Printed in the United States of America

0718 1P CGF18

Table of Contents

Police Dogs

Dogs are man's best friend. They are also good friends to the police. Dogs help the police catch a **suspect**. They can track down a missing person. They can even find dangerous things like bombs or guns. How?

Police dogs work at airports and important buildings. They help keep us safe.

Dogs can smell 40–50 times better than we can. They can also hear four times better. Plus, dogs are very smart and learn quickly. But, they need special training.

German Shepherds, Beagles, Bloodhounds, and Labradors make good police dogs.

It takes months to train police dogs. They are trained by one person—their handler. This police officer will become their best friend. The officer uses treats to teach a dog. When the dog's work is done, it goes to live with the officer's family.

Firefighter Dogs

Firefighters also use dogs to help them. These dogs are called **arson** dogs. They are trained to sniff out the cause of a fire. These dogs are so good, they can work faster than a machine!

Arson dogs go to school for three months. They learn to **detect** sixty different things that can start a fire. What do they do when they find one? They sit down, look at the firefighter, and put their nose where the smell can be found.

You can find a National Fire Dog Monument in Washington D.C. Each year an award is given to a hero dog around the country. These arson dogs also visit schools to teach kids about fire safety.

National Fire Dog Monument in Washington, D.C.

ENGINE CO
RESCUE CO

"ASHES TO ANSWERS"
SCULPTED BY
AUSTIN WEISHEL
NATIONAL FIRE DOG MONUMENT

Other Animal Detectives

Pigs like to oink and play in the mud. But did you know pigs can be good detectives, too? For a long time, pigs have been used to find truffles in the forest. But, a pig's great sense of smell can be used for so much more!

Truffles are a special kind of mushroom.

Pigs have been trained to find bombs. You might spot one sniffing around at an airport. In some countries, pigs are also used to sniff out land mines left behind after a war. Mines can blow up and hurt people.

Good to Know

Pigs and wild boars have a better sense of smell than dogs! These helpers save hundreds of lives each year.

A pig's snout can smell better than our nose!

Like pigs, bees have good senses. You've probably seen a honeybee flying around a flower. It is using its senses to find the flower's sweet nectar. That's a tasty treat for a bee. But bees can be trained to find something else.

Bees have been taught to find land mines too. Since bees weigh so little, they can find a mine without it blowing up. This saves people from getting hurt. So the next time you swat away a bee, remember...it could be on a special mission!

What mission could this bee be on?

Words to Keep

arson: the act of setting a fire to something
detect: to discover or find something
suspect: someone who police wish to talk to about a crime

Learn More at the Library

Books (Check out these books to learn more.)

Bee Detectives by Rosie Albright. PowerKids Press, 2012.

Pig Detectives by Rosie Albright. PowerKids Press, 2012.

Sadie: The Dog Who Finds the Evidence (Ready-to-Read) by Thea Feldman. Simon Spotlight, 2014.

Web Sites (Ask an adult to show you these web sites.)

American Humane Hero Awards:
www.herodogawards.org

Pet Heroes: Sabre the Police Dog (YouTube)
https://www.youtube.com/watch?v=bCQAb1LIFpU

Index

About the Author

Wiley Blevins has taught elementary school in the United States and South America. He has also written over 75 books for children. He keeps an eye out for animal detectives in his New York City neighborhood.